Balance

by

Robbi Nester

ISBN-13: 978-0615607078 ISBN-10: 0615607071

Artwork by Nina Canal

Cover photo by John Genesta

White Violet Press

1840 W. 220th Street Suite 300
Torrance, Calif. 90501

Dedication

To Richard, with love and gratitude,
and to all my teachers, including but not limited to
Richard Dillard, Denise Thibault, Karin O'Bannon, Bob Metzler
and their teachers. And to Mr. B.K.S. Iyengar for developing
this yoga that has enriched my life.

Table of Contents

Adho Mukha Svanasana

In my father's cellar, full of
bric a brac, oscilloscopes
once hummed, energy
made visible, pictures of sound.
A god of volts and ohms, I'd
turn the knobs until the line
reared up, became an inchworm.
Now that energy is in me.
The legs, like oaks, bear all
their secret life beneath the skin.
The spine stretches toward
the immaterial, while the head,
though distant as the moon, wants
only to rest itself against the knees.

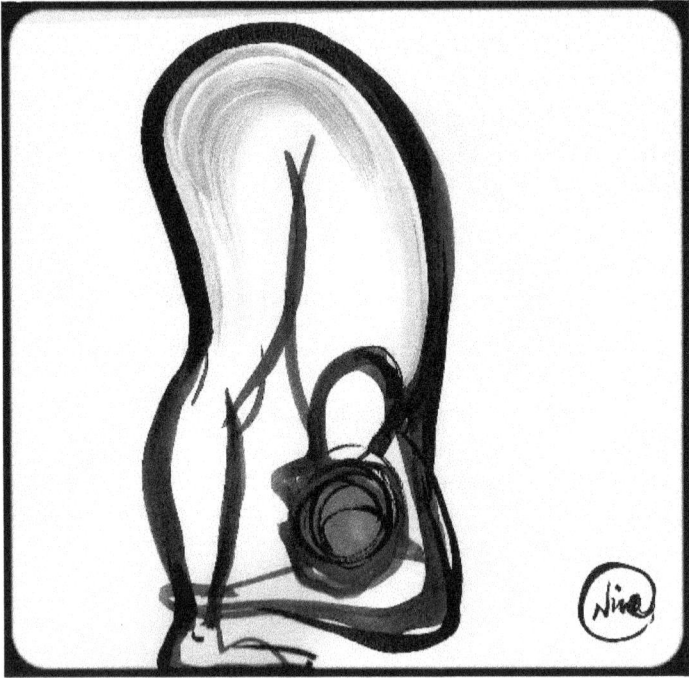

Uttanasana

Diving down and down
toward the distant floor,
I approach the knees'
locked gates, peering
into the darkened space
between, almost at my
destination. Grasping
the heels, the ropy
tendons, I belly forward.
Chest presses thighs,
buttocks rising and rising.
I am an explorer,
entering the ancient city,
descending into another world.

Salamba Sirsanana

The moon swells like a seedpod.
Inside the quiet studio, I take
my aching head into my hands,
fingers web to web. A breath,
and then this awkward frame
ascends, becomes an aspen,
flexing in a nonexistent breeze.
Grounded in air, movement merges
with stillness, my ear a vehicle
for surging tides, the galaxies'
faint hum. Everywhere
and nowhere, the worlds
fall away, balanced
on these two arms

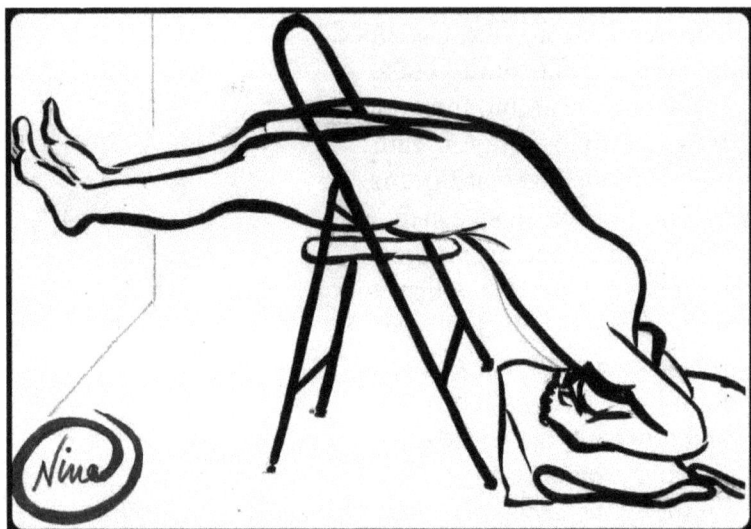

Viparita Dandasana

In this pose, I am a child again,
arcing backwards from the old
brown couch. The ordinary room,
with its worn black rug, scattered
with pink roses like none that grew
out in the yard, became a reef
crowned with the tiny,
pulsing mouths of coral,
their home a crypt and nursery,
built on the others' bones.
The T.V.'s featureless face
gave back my own face, turned
alien and odd, and I, a curious
dolphin, weightless and free.

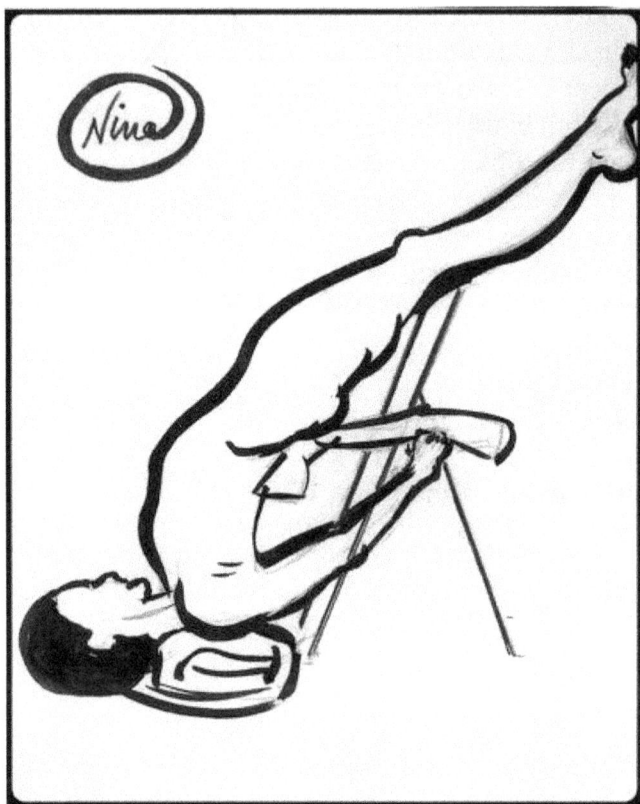

Sarvangasana

Inside its shell, all martial turrets,
spiral points, the whelk,
soft as a tongue, slips unhindered
through the polished rose-pink
lips, while I, creature
of another sea, head downward
on this chair, extend
my toes like pink-tipped
tentacles. My head is free
for once to lose its lofty
place, and pillowed
on the floor, looks only
inwards at the chest, hands
lightly grasping the back bar.

Niralamba Sarvangasana

The earth hangs in space.
No guide wires, not even
the thinnest, suspend
this green-blue bauble
from the sky. My body
also has its gravity, propelled
by breath, unfurling
like a fiddlehead,
head down and backward,
open fingers grasping
only air. If breath
should flutter, I would fail
instead of folding
inward, like a snail

Niralamba Halasana

These blades cut deep,
carving out a cave
from legs and torso,
where intestines'
pearly ropes fall free,
and the heart, suspended,
beats its regular tattoo
against the chest until
the vaulted rafters ring.
The lungs—two sails—
spread their manta wings,
and breath bears me down
through the sweet darkness,
all the way to the end

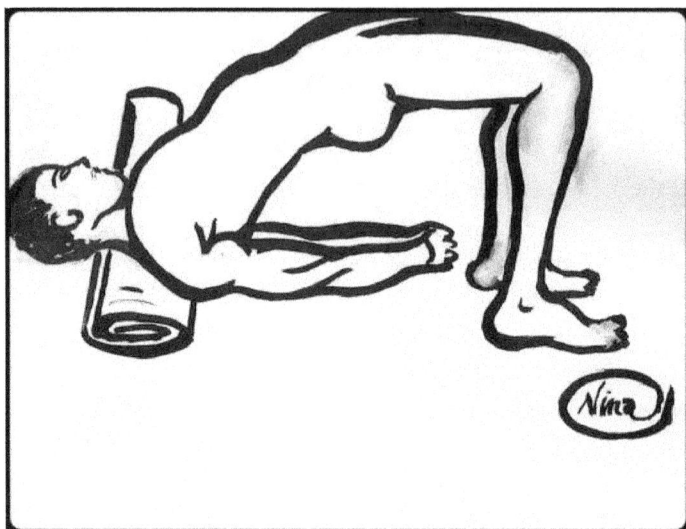

Setubandha Sarvangasana

On this cold floor, hoisting
my hips, I am standing
in the canyon, waiting
for the full moon to rise.
And now, the sky, so
empty in the daylight,
swells full of secrets,
like a darkened hall
before the concert starts.
Till a thin sliver of light,
golden, almost a sound,
skims the rock, and the moon,
with a clash of cymbals,
breaks free of the canyon walls.

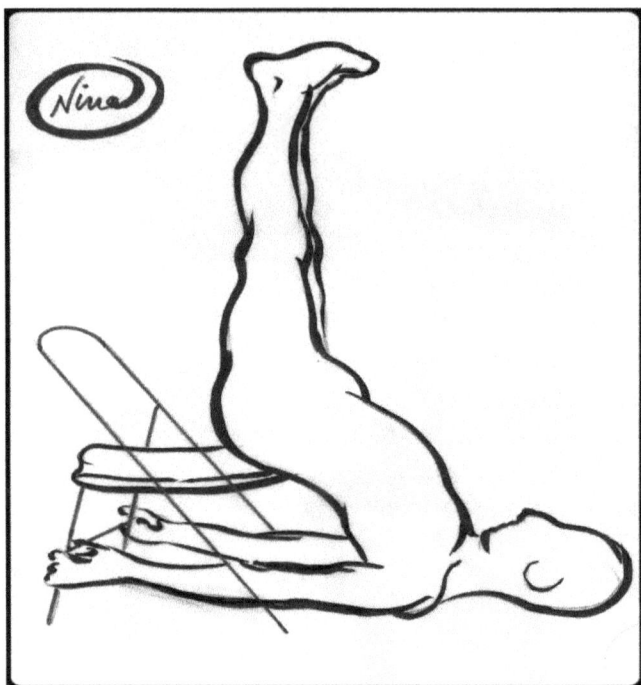

Viparita Karani in Sarvangasana

Force arises in surprising places.
The seed knows its strength—
an insistent shoot will crack
the brittle shell, find a way
out of the hard-packed earth.
And the rain, in pinprick
drops, breaks off bits
from the towering nimbus,
wearing down mountains
and turning rocks to sand.
It is not muscle that raises
my legs from the chair,
but a gathering force,
like flame from a struck match.

Paschimottanasana

I am rowing my boat
along the quiet river.
My ribs open like a magnolia
flower, its stiff white petals
only this morning furled
in the burnished bud.
Legs strung tight as sails,
I hoist myself up, out of the hip,
arranging my torso, vessel
of precious cargo, over the knees.
Currents lap at my sides
as I surge forward, pulling
the oars of my feet
till the miles fall away.

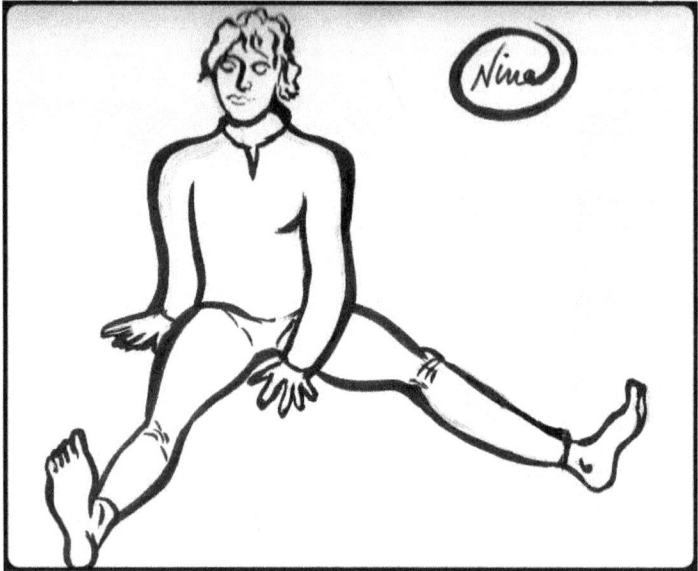

Upavista Konasana

At the reptile house I watched
with curiosity a black snake
with two heads, one head straining
to the left, the other straight,
a strategy that failed.
In this pose, each leg
stretches its own way,
parsing space like calipers,
and yet the spine, braided
through with thorns, becomes
a stem to hold all wayward
parts in check. I bow, pale
bloom nodding in a breeze,
honoring each leg in turn.

Baddhakonasana

These feet have seldom met.
All lifetime long, fated to tread
their single paths on yielding earth,
to press parched soles against
unsympathetic streets, they
desire only new routes, never
dreaming what they truly seek.
Yet arch to arch, each toe
pressing its long-lost opposite,
these feet have met their match.
Bound in a forced embrace, they find
a blessing in this union, welded
in a prayer to all things lost,
to what was always there.

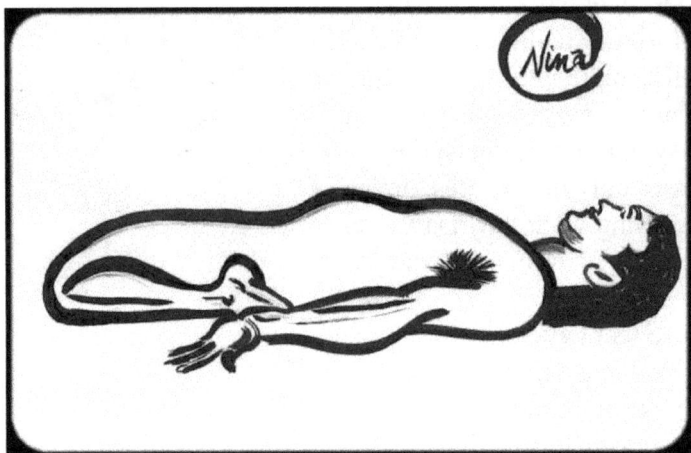

Supta Virasana

On the road to the studio, the hills
undulate under the clouds like fish
in the shallows, soft morning light
singing on their silver scales.
I want to lie down in that light
and become a hill, but my mind
won't let me. Let me try again
to still the muscles' long
sigh as legs enfold the hips,
tucked under like hospital corners,
the thighs pulled taut as a harp string,
the ribs pried open as I
lie back on the folded blankets
exposing my heart to the world.

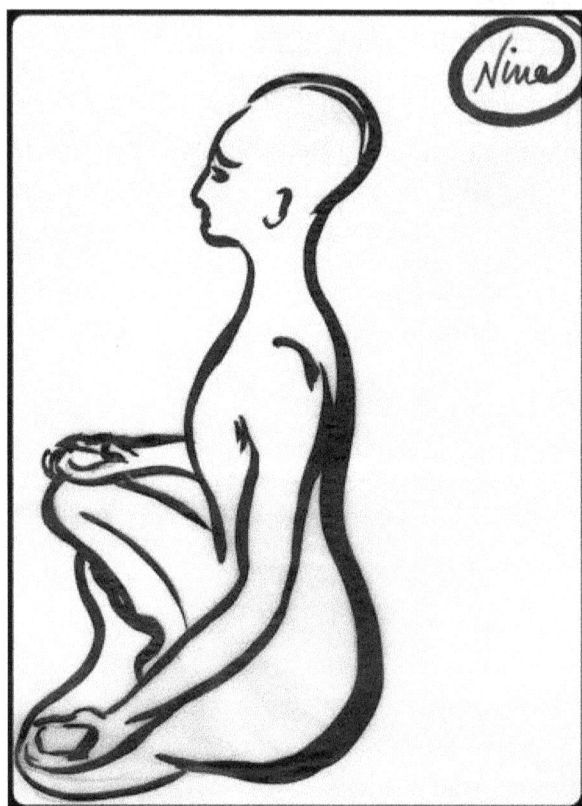

Viloma Pranayama

In the quiet darkness, the stately
planets prance, wheeling in their
orbits, like partners in a dance.
The sun inspects its minions,
reclining on its throne. Mars, then Venus
passes until earth stands alone.
It bows before his majesty, low,
then lower, lowest. It seems to
bite off brightness, in incremental bits,
so that it shrinks to one bright line
and finally disappears. For me,
beneath the coral tree, a thousand
shadows mass, ghostly-green
coronas, wavering on the path.

Savasana

It is late night in the desert.
Miles of cool highway
slip by in the dark.
Thin saguaros, tall as a man,
stand watch by the roadside,
their arms full of blossoms
gathered in the night, haunted
by pale Luna moths, the color
of twilight. In a sky deep
as breath, a circus of stars
tumbles and twirls, though
no one is watching, not even
me. Along the spine of the sleeping
mountains, the white line glows.

Biography

Robbi Nester lives, writes, and practices yoga in Southern California. Her work has appeared in the anthologies Easy to Love but Hard to Raise (DRT Press) and Flashlight Memories (Silver Boomer Press), and she has published her poetry in Qarrtsiluni, Victorian Violet Press, Inlandia, Floyd County Moonshine, and Caesura.

9 780615 607078